P9-DJU-968

347.9

I KNOW AMERICA

Our Supreme Court

Meish Goldish

THE MILLBROOK PRESS

Brookfield, Connecticut

BENNETT-HEMENWAY
SCHOOL LIBRARY
NATICK, MA

Published by The Millbrook Press
2 Old New Milford Road
Brookfield, CT 06804
© 1994 Blackbirch Graphics, Inc.

All rights reserved. No part of this book may be reproduced in any form
without the permission in writing from the publisher except by a reviewer.
Printed in the United States of America.

10 9 8 7 6 5 4 3 2 1

Created and produced in association with Blackbirch Graphics.
Series Editor: Tanya Lee Stone

Library of Congress Cataloging-in-Publication Data
Goldish, Meish
  Our Supreme Court / Meish Goldish.
    p.   cm. — (I know America)
  Includes bibliographical references and index.
  Summary: Describes the history, powers, and makeup of the Supreme Court and
how a case makes its way to the Supreme Court through the state or federal system.
    ISBN 1-56294-445-2
    1. United States. Supreme Court—History—Juvenile literature. [1. United States.
2. Supreme Court.] I. Title. II. Series.
KF8742.Z9G65   1994
347.73'26—dc20
[347.30735]   94-7640
                                                                          CIP
                                                                          AC

Photo Credits
Cover: ©Bruce Hoertel/Gamma Liaison; pp. 5, 19, 22: North Wind Picture
Archives; pp. 6, 9, 11, 13, 30, 36: ©Blackbirch Press, Inc.; pp. 10, 20, 28,
33, 35, 37: Collection of the Supreme Court of the United States; p. 14:
National Portrait Gallery; p. 17: Vic Boswell/Collection of the Supreme
Court of the United States; p.21: ©The National Geographic Society,
Courtesy, The Supreme Court Historical Society; pp. 32, 38: Wide World
Photos, Inc.; pp. 42, 44: AP/Wide World Photos.

CONTENTS

The Supreme Court is known as the highest court in the land. Not even the president has more power than the Supreme Court, which serves as the interpreter of the U.S. Constitution. A legal case that has passed through the lower courts can be appealed to the Supreme Court only if it involves an important constitutional question.

The Supreme Court can overturn (change) a lower court's ruling if it decides that the ruling is unconstitutional—that is, if the ruling goes against the Constitution. Once the Court rules, all other courts in the country must rule the same way in similar cases. A decision of the Supreme Court sets a precedent (an action that serves as an example). This precedent must be followed by all lower courts.

The nine justices who make up the Court are appointed by the president and approved by the

This 1890 engraving illustrates the interior chamber of the Supreme Court.

Senate. The rulings they make are final, unless the Court itself changes its mind.

Since 1790, the Supreme Court has helped to shape American society. Its decisions affect every aspect of our lives—at home, at work, and at school. By interpreting the Constitution and applying it to our laws, the Supreme Court helps guarantee equal justice for everyone in the United States.

PURPOSE AND POWERS OF THE COURT

In the dictionary, the word *supreme* is defined as "highest in rank or power." It makes sense, therefore, that our most powerful court should be called the Supreme Court.

The idea of a Supreme Court came from the writers of the Constitution of the United States in 1787. They created our nation's basic laws. Article III of the Constitution says: "The judicial power of the United States shall be vested [placed] in one Supreme Court, and in such inferior courts as the Congress may from time to time...establish."

Inferior courts are courts that are lower in rank than the Supreme Court. These courts are also very important. They are where almost all cases are first heard and decided. If a person is accused of murder, for example, the case begins in a lower court.

Opposite:
"Equal Justice Under Law" is inscribed on the Supreme Court building in Washington, D.C., and is the basis of our judicial system.

Under American law, however, people who lose their cases in court can appeal (ask a higher court to hear their case again). If the appeal is granted, they go to a higher court. People often want to appeal because there is a possibility that a higher court may rule differently than the lower court did. If it does, the first ruling is overturned, or rejected. The new ruling then stands. The highest court that can be appealed to is the Supreme Court of the United States.

There are very few cases that ever actually reach the Supreme Court. The Court does not have the time needed to judge every case it is asked to hear. Out of about 5,000 requests the Supreme Court receives each year, it accepts only about 175 cases. Supreme Court judges have to make their choices by considering only those cases that involve an important constitutional question.

The Job of the Court

The Supreme Court does not create the laws of our country. That is the function of the legislature, or lawmakers. Every year, new laws are proposed and passed by local governments, state governments, and the federal government.

One of the jobs of the Supreme Court is to interpret any new laws that are questioned, or old laws that are challenged, in order to determine whether or not they violate the Constitution. To do that, the Supreme Court uses the Constitution of the United States as its guide.

Interpreting the Law

The language in the Constitution is not always clear. Sometimes the meanings of words or phrases are interpreted or understood differently by people. The Supreme Court decides the meaning of the Constitution and then determines if a law is unconstitutional.

Here's an example of how the Supreme Court interprets a law: Suppose your town passed a new law saying that anyone who speaks insultingly of the town will be arrested and put into jail. Although the purpose of that law may be to promote local pride, many people would say such a law is unconstitutional. Why? Because our Constitution says that Americans have freedom of speech. This includes our right to insult our own town. If the new law was challenged, the Supreme Court would declare it to be unconstitutional based on freedom of speech.

The U.S. Constitution is used by the Court as a guide for interpreting laws.

But how far does freedom of speech extend? Suppose a person shouted "Fire!" in a movie theater as a joke. The crowd would rush out, and people might get hurt. When the person who yelled "Fire!" was arrested, he or she could claim, "I've broken no law! The Constitution says I have freedom of speech!"

Do you agree? The Supreme Court would not, because of the harm the statement could cause. One of the Court's most famous judges, Oliver Wendell Holmes, once wrote: "The most stringent [strict] protection of free speech would not protect a man in falsely shouting fire in a theater and causing a panic."

Oliver Wendell Holmes served as a Supreme Court justice for almost thirty years.

Everyone Obeys the Supreme Court

A decision made by the Supreme Court is very powerful. Even the president of the United States cannot ignore a Supreme Court decision. In 1952, President Harry S. Truman feared that workers in our nation's steel mills were about to go on strike. He ordered the secretary of commerce to take over the mills to keep them operating. But the Supreme Court said that the mills were private property. It ruled that Truman's takeover was unconstitutional. The president had to obey the Court's decision, and the takeover was ended.

In 1974, a judge ordered President Richard Nixon to hand over tape recordings of White House meetings. They were wanted as evidence in a government investigation. Nixon refused. He said that the Constitution gave the president executive privilege—the right to keep records private. After losing in the U.S. Court of Appeals, Nixon appealed to the Supreme Court. It agreed with the lower court and declared that executive privilege has limits. The president then turned over the tapes.

In 1952, the Supreme Court ruled that President Harry S. Truman's attempt to control privately operated steel mills was unconstitutional.

How Rulings Are Changed

Despite the Supreme Court's power, there are two ways its rulings can be changed. One way is if the Court itself decides to rethink its ruling. The Supreme Court can review a case that may be similar to a past one and make a ruling that overturns the earlier decision.

11

Why would the Court ever change its mind? This sometimes happens when our nation's attitudes also change. For example, before the 1950s, many states would not allow African Americans and whites to attend the same public schools. The Supreme Court said that was legal. But in 1954, the Court changed its mind. Over the years, our nation had changed its thinking about racial segregation. The Court's 1954 decision reflected that change.

The second way a Supreme Court ruling can be changed is by an amendment. Amendments to the Constitution are proposed by the Senate and the House of Representatives. Getting these additional laws passed is a long and hard process. But when it

THE BRANCHES OF GOVERNMENT

Who is in charge of our laws? The government is, and the task is very large. So the government has three branches, or divisions, and each branch performs a different job.

The legislative branch is responsible for making the laws. We have lawmakers for individual towns, for states, and for the federal government. The lawmakers for our federal government are the members of Congress (the Senate and the House of Representatives).

The executive branch carries out the laws. The executive branch also has the right to reject laws that Congress wants to pass. This branch is headed by the president, who is also the commander-in-chief of the armed forces.

The judicial branch judges the laws. It decides if laws are fair or not. The judicial branch encompasses all of our courts, including the Supreme Court.

happens, the Supreme Court uses the amendment as a new guide for making its decisions.

    For example, when the Constitution was first written, it allowed the states to determine who could vote in elections. However, throughout the years amendments to the Constitution changed this. The Fifteenth Amendment, ratified (approved) in 1870, said states could not deny the right to vote to former slaves. The Nineteenth Amendment, ratified in 1920, stopped the states from denying the vote to women, and in 1971, the Twenty-sixth Amendment secured the vote for all citizens over the age of eighteen.

Suffragettes, women who campaigned for their right to vote, gathered in 1914 at the Congressional Union for Woman's Suffrage in Newport, Rhode Island.

A HISTORY OF THE COURT

The Supreme Court has existed for more than 200 years. During that time, the Court has changed in many ways. Some of its earliest decisions may not seem very remarkable to us today. But that's because we now take for granted the powers that the Court established in its early years.

A Shaky Start

The Supreme Court had an uncertain beginning. President George Washington appointed six justices to the Court (as opposed to the nine we have today). However, at the Court's first session on February 1, 1790, only three justices were present. When a fourth arrived the next day, it was discovered that there weren't any matters to discuss, and the "session" quickly ended.

Opposite:
Chief Justice John Marshall led and helped to shape the Supreme Court for more than thirty years.

In 1793, the Supreme Court handed down one of its first major decisions and declared that the citizens of South Carolina had the right to sue the state of Georgia. Just five years later, Americans adopted the Eleventh Amendment, making it illegal for one state to sue another state. This made the powers of the new Supreme Court seem very weak at first.

There are several reasons why the Court did not remain weak. Presidents and members of Congress could be voted out of office, but not Supreme Court justices. They were given lifetime jobs and were able to act freely on issues, regardless of public opinion.

Second, the Constitution was not perfectly clear about how much power the Supreme Court really had. Article III merely stated: "Judicial power shall extend to all cases...arising under this constitution." But those words prompted many questions: Could the Court only settle arguments between states? Could it also reject laws passed by Congress? The answers came in 1803, in one of the Court's most historic cases.

Marbury v. *Madison*

In 1800, John Adams lost the presidential election. In 1801, before he left office, he appointed John Marshall to be chief justice. He also appointed justices of the peace in the nation's new capital, Washington, D.C. One of those appointed was William Marbury. But, when Adams left office on March 3, 1801, Marbury had not received the official paper—known as a commission—that he needed to hold office.

On March 4, 1801, Thomas Jefferson took office. Marbury asked the new secretary of state, James Madison, for his commission. Jefferson was very angry that Adams had appointed so many of his friends, like Marbury, to jobs. So Jefferson told Madison to ignore Marbury's request. Marbury then decided to sue to get his commission. The case is called *Marbury* v. *Madison*.

Chief Justice Marshall and President Jefferson had very different views about how the government should be run, but the Court had a case to decide. Marshall feared that Jefferson would simply ignore the Court's decision if it favored Marbury. If its decision was ignored by the president, the Court would look weak and powerless.

James Madison (left) was sued by William Marbury (right) in 1801. *Marbury* v. *Madison* resulted in the Supreme Court's power to declare federal laws unconstitutional.

HOW CASES ARE TITLED

Supreme Court cases get their titles by using the names of the two sides involved. The first name is the person or group who lost in the lower court and is bringing the appeal. The second name is the lower-court winner, who is now defending the lower-court ruling.

For example, suppose Smith lost to Jones in the lower court and is now bringing the case to the Supreme Court. That case would be titled *Smith* v. *Jones*. The "v." in the title stands for versus, meaning against.

One side in a Supreme Court case may be a state. In a murder case, for example, the state brings charges against the accused. In an appeal, the case would have a title such as *Johnson* v. *North Carolina*.

If a person is suing the federal government, or appealing a criminal conviction, the case would have a title such as *Robinson* v. *United States*.

But Chief Justice Marshall was clever. In his decision, he said Marbury's case should not be heard by the Supreme Court. Congress had passed a law giving the Court that right, but the Constitution never gave Congress the right to make such a law. Since Congress's law went against the Constitution, said Marshall, it could not stand, and in 1803 he ruled against Marbury.

The case established that the Supreme Court had the power to declare laws of Congress unconstitutional. That power became known as judicial review.

Today, the Court still has the power of judicial review. It can reject a law of Congress that it finds to be in conflict with the Constitution.

The Court Grows in Power

After the Marbury case, the Supreme Court grew in power and respect. During the 1800s, other important decisions were made by the Court. Many involved business and industry. In one ruling, *Gibbons* v. *Ogden*, the Court held that states could not give one person the sole right to run steamboats to other states. Another ruling, *The Dartmouth College Case*, stopped the state of New Hampshire from forcing a private college to become a state college.

Other Supreme Court rulings involved people's individual and civil rights. One historic case was *Dred Scott* v. *Sandford* in 1857. The Court's decision in this case shook the nation and helped to bring about the Civil War.

The Dred Scott Case

Dred Scott was an African-American slave in Missouri. In the 1830s, his master had taken him to the territory that later became Minnesota. Congress had banned slavery in this territory in an 1820 law known as the Missouri Compromise. Scott sued for freedom and argued that the Missouri Compromise made him free when his master took him to Minnesota.

The Supreme Court made a terrible ruling. Chief Justice Roger B. Taney stated that because Scott was an African American, he could never be an American citizen and had no right to sue in a U.S. federal court. Taney also declared it unconstitutional for Congress to ban slavery in any of the western territories.

In 1857, Dred Scott sued for his freedom and lost.

Americans who were against slavery were angered by the Court's decision. Four years later, the Civil War began. In the end, Dred Scott was given his freedom by a new master.

The Dred Scott case is an example of how a Constitutional amendment can overrule a Supreme Court decision. In 1868, the nation passed the Fourteenth Amendment, which stated that all persons who were born in the United States were citizens. The amendment also prohibited the state from denying equal rights to Americans. Starting in the 1940s, the Court used this amendment to give blacks and other minorities equal justice under the law.

THE LOCATION OF THE SUPREME COURT

The location of the Supreme Court has changed many times during its early history. In 1790, the Court's first two meetings were held in the Royal Exchange Building in New York City.

The Royal Exchange Building in New York City.

When our nation's capital moved to Philadelphia in 1791, the Court moved there, too. It first met in Liberty Hall, before changing to Old City Hall.

In 1801, our capital was established in Washington, D.C. The Court moved to be in the capital city. It originally used rooms in the Capitol Building until receiving its permanent home, the Supreme Court Building, in 1935.

The Changing Number of Justices

The Supreme Court has changed in other ways over the years. In 1790, the first Court had only six justices. Later, the number was increased to nine. Still later, it became ten, and then seven. But in 1869, the number of justices returned to nine and it has stayed there ever since.

In the 1930s, President Franklin Roosevelt tried to get a new law passed. It would have increased the total number of Supreme Court justices to fifteen. Roosevelt wanted to fill the Court with judges whose political views agreed with his own. But Congress rejected the idea. It felt that "packing" the Court would weaken its reputation for honesty and fairness.

The 1993 Supreme Court. Standing from left: Clarence Thomas, Anthony Kennedy, David H. Souter, and Ruth Bader Ginsburg. Seated from left: Sandra Day O'Connor, Harry A. Blackmun, William Rehnquist, Byron White, and Antonin Scalia.

C H A P T E R

3

HOW THE COURT OPERATES

The Supreme Court is made up of eight associate justices and one chief justice, who is the Court's leader. Associate justices earn $159,600 a year. The chief justice earns $166,200 because the job has extra duties.

The Supreme Court does not have time to hear every case that is brought before it. It chooses cases involving the most important legal and constitutional issues. At least four of the nine justices must agree to hear a case before it is accepted.

Occasionally, Congress may order the Supreme Court to review a case. But usually a case is brought by the losing side in a lower court. Suppose a man is found guilty of a murder in a lower court. After the verdict, the man claims that the judge made an error in handling the trial. He says his constitutional rights

Opposite:
Chief Justice Salmon Chase and associates hear arguments in a Supreme Court case in 1867.

23

to a fair trial were denied. The Supreme Court might decide to hear the case, if it believes it involves a key issue about the Constitution.

In another example, suppose a company is sued by the government for not paying a federal tax. After losing in lower court, the company still feels that the tax law is unfair. The Supreme Court might agree to hear that case, since it involves federal law.

Arguing a Case

Appearing before the Supreme Court is a great honor for the lawyers who represent both sides of a case. Today, if a case involves the U.S. government, one of the lawyers is usually the solicitor general of the United States. Lawyers who argue cases before the Court must state their arguments in writing and stand before the nine justices to explain their views aloud, answering questions from the judges.

Despite the great importance of a Supreme Court case, the hearing is very informal. There are no witnesses and no jury in the chamber. Lawyers for each side are usually given thirty minutes to present their arguments. As they speak, justices may interrupt to ask them questions about the case. Later, after all arguments have been presented, the justices consider the issue, discuss the case, and come to a decision.

Making a Decision

At a justices' meeting (held in secrecy), the chief justice starts the discussion. Each justice is asked to

give his or her opinion. Then the justices take a vote.
Each of them, including the chief justice, has only one
vote. They do not have to be in complete agreement,
and often they are not. The majority rules, meaning
that since there are nine justices, the opinion held by
five or more becomes the Court's official decision in
the case.

If the chief justice agrees with the majority, he
or she either writes the opinion or assigns it to an
associate justice to write. If the chief justice is not in
the majority, then the justice in the majority who has
been on the Supreme Court the longest either writes
the opinion or assigns it to someone else to write.
This is known as the "majority opinion" or the
"opinion of the Court." All of the justices are free to
write their own opinions explaining exactly why they
agree with the majority opinion or why they disagree.
These are called concurring opinions and dissenting
opinions.

The writing of Supreme Court decisions is done
with special care. Justices want their opinions to be
clear to everyone who reads them. They know that all
lower courts will use their decisions as guidelines for
similar cases.   Justice Louis Brandeis once wrote forty-
three drafts of an opinion before he felt it was worded
exactly right.

Each decision is read aloud in the Court. It is
also published in a Supreme Court record called *The
United States Reports.* Newspapers also often publish
the decisions.

THE PATHWAYS OF JUSTICE

Our judicial system has many courts. They fall into two general categories: state courts and federal courts. State courts use state laws as their guide. Federal courts use federal laws and the Constitution.

Most cases are heard in state courts. A case starts in a state, or trial, court with a jury if there has been a violation of a state law, or if it is a case between people who live in the same state. State court cases usually include cases for property damage, robbery, or murder. If the person who loses can show that the trial court unfairly affected the decision, the case can be appealed in a State Supreme Court. In this situation, the case is not tried again in front of a jury. Instead, the decision of the trial court is reviewed. Sometimes, a case may question the constitutionality of a law and be appealed again in the U.S. Supreme Court.

Other cases are heard in federal courts. Any violation of a federal law, such as mail theft or counterfeiting, or any lawsuit between residents of different states, is heard in the federal court. A case can then be appealed in the U.S. Court of Appeals, which uses the same procedure that the State Supreme Court does. If an area of constitutional law is being disputed, or if there have been different rulings on similar cases in the past, the case may be appealed in the U.S. Supreme Court.

Many cases can be divided into two basic categories: civil cases and criminal cases. In a civil case, one person or group sues another person or group over a private matter such as property damage, contracts, divorce, or personal injury. For example, a landlord may sue a tenant for not paying rent. In most civil cases, the person who sues seeks money as payment for the damage done.

In a criminal case, the state or federal government brings charges against a person or group for an action that is harmful to society. Criminal cases often involve serious crimes against people, such as murder, assault, and kidnapping. They may also deal with crimes against property, such as arson, car theft, burglary, or vandalism. In a criminal case, the government wants the convicted person or group punished, usually with a fine, a prison sentence, or both.

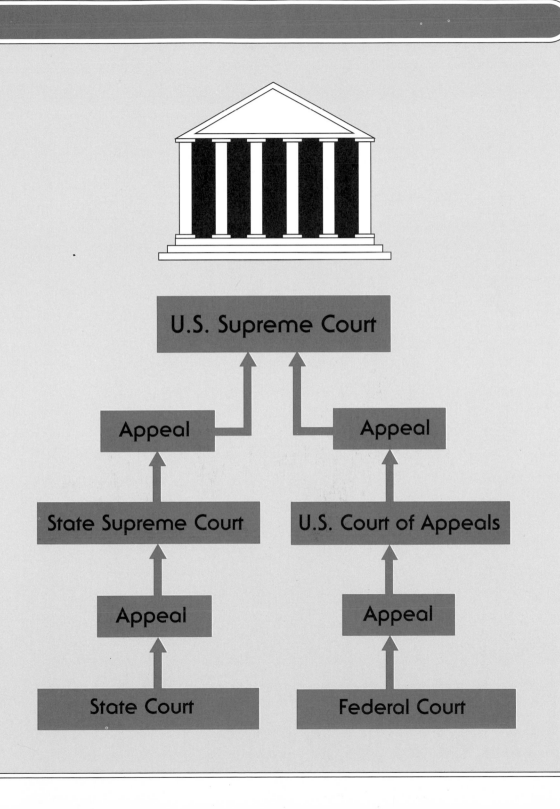

The Work Calendar

The Supreme Court begins its term or work year on the first Monday in October. The term usually ends the following June, but may go later if the Court has not completed all its work by then.

Even during the summer break, the justices are not entirely free. They are constantly reviewing requests for cases to be heard in the coming term. Sometimes cases are so important that they meet in the summer to hear them.

Because of their huge workload, justices are given special help. Each justice has a secretary, a messenger, and several law clerks. Each law clerk usually works for one year. They help do legal research and prepare written opinions.

The Supreme Court chamber. Visitors can watch attorneys present cases to the justices in this room.

VISITING THE SUPREME COURT

The Supreme Court works in the Supreme Court Building in Washington, D.C. On the marble wall outside, it reads: "Equal Justice Under the Law." This is a reminder that the Court shows no favors or bias toward either side in a case.

The Supreme Court Building is open to the public. More than 500,000 visitors pass through each year. People are allowed to hear the Court in session. There are chairs and benches for about 300 visitors in the courtroom. Another section of the room is reserved for news reporters and for guests of the Court. Getting seats can be hard, especially for the most important cases.

The justices are behind a long desk called "the bench." They sit on nine black chairs of differing heights. The chairs don't match because when justices join the Court they are allowed to choose from several types of chairs. In the middle of the bench is the chief justice's chair.

The Court calendar is divided into two-week sittings and two-week recesses. During the sittings, the Court hears cases. During the recesses, the justices consider each case, do research, and write their opinions.

The day that is chosen for deciding cases as a group is usually a Friday. All of the justices meet in a conference room for their discussion. However, before they begin to talk, they always carry on an old tradition of first shaking hands with one another. It reminds them that even though they might disagree in their opinions, a sense of harmony must always rule over the Supreme Court.

C H A P T E R

4

FAMOUS SUPREME COURT JUSTICES

Since the beginning, in 1790, the Supreme Court has had a total of over 100 justices. Many became famous for their work in the Court, as well as in other areas of their lives.

Requirements for Justices

Becoming a Supreme Court justice is a great honor. Justices are appointed by the president of the United States, and then the Senate must approve their appointment.

      Over the years, there have been times when the Senate did not approve a president's choice for the Supreme Court. Members of the Senate felt that that person would not make a good Supreme Court justice. The president then had to submit another name.

Opposite:
This illustration of former chief justices of the Supreme Court was created in 1894.

31

MAKING THE GRADE

Robert Bork was rejected as a Supreme Court nominee.

Being asked to join the Supreme Court sometimes comes as a surprise. The president may telephone the person chosen and say, "Would you like to be nominated as a Supreme Court justice?" Often the nominee is a colleague of the president who shares the same political views. Because of the importance of the justice's job, the president makes the choice very carefully.

But being nominated to the Supreme Court is half the battle.

Justices cannot join the Supreme Court unless a majority of the Senate approves, or "confirms." The Senate takes a vote after holding public meetings called "hearings." At these hearings, Senate members ask the nominee about his or her political views and beliefs. Political groups also try to influence the Senate members' votes. They write letters, make phone calls, hold rallies, and take out newspaper advertisements. Like the president and senators, they too want a justice whose political views agree with their own.

In the past, most—but not all—nominees have been confirmed to serve on the Court. In 1969 and 1970, two of President Nixon's choices for the Court were rejected before Harry Blackmun was finally accepted. In 1987, one of President Reagan's choices, Robert Bork, was rejected by the Senate. Many of the senators felt his political views were too conservative for the good of the country. The following year, Anthony Kennedy was confirmed instead.

There are no rules about who qualifies as a Supreme Court justice. Often, justices have worked previously as lawyers or as judges in lower courts. Once appointed, justices may serve on the Supreme Court for the rest of their lives.

The Congress has the power to remove a justice from the bench through impeachment (charges against a public official for crime or misconduct) by the House of Representatives and conviction (finding someone guilty of the charges) by the Senate. But in the Court's entire history this has never happened.

When a justice resigns, retires, or dies, the president chooses a replacement. If the chief justice leaves, an associate justice may be given the job. Then a new associate is named. The president can also decide to name an outsider to the Court to be the new chief justice.

Notable Chief Justices

John Jay

John Jay served from 1790 to 1795 as the first chief justice of the Supreme Court. His belief in a strong federal government was shared by President George Washington, who appointed him.

Before joining the Court, Jay showed that he was a great diplomat. After the Revolutionary War, he worked out a peace treaty with England. He also helped to get the Constitution ratified. After leaving the Supreme Court, Jay became governor of New York.

John Jay was a diplomat before becoming the first chief justice in 1790.

One of Jay's main accomplishments as chief justice was the creation of the Jay Treaty. It settled arguments between the United States and England over shipping and trading rights. Overall, Jay's courage and intelligence helped to establish our Supreme Court.

John Marshall

John Marshall earned the title of "Great Chief Justice" on the Supreme Court. When he accepted the job in 1801, the Supreme Court did not command very much attention or respect. But during Marshall's thirty-four years of leadership, the Court increased in power and dignity. The "Marshall Court," as it came to be known, handed down thousands of important decisions.

Earl Warren

Earl Warren served as chief justice for sixteen years from 1953 to 1969. He was known as a free-thinking individual with strong beliefs. He worked especially hard to guarantee justice for poor people and minorities.

Under Warren, the Supreme Court expanded the liberties of all American citizens. Warren promoted free speech, religious freedom, and fairness for racial and ethnic groups. Under his leadership, the Court outlawed all racial segregation in the country and guaranteed that all people would have a lawyer if they were arrested.

Notable Associate Justices

Oliver Wendell Holmes

For nearly thirty years, starting in 1902, Oliver Wendell Holmes served with great distinction on the Court. He became known as "The Great Dissenter," because he often disagreed with the other justices. Holmes believed that courts should not interfere with lawmakers if at all possible. He often urged the other justices not to let their personal feelings affect their decisions. He believed in relying on reason and logic in the decision-making process.

Holmes strongly favored people's rights. He felt that laws needed to be changed as people's needs also changed. He believed that the Constitution is a "living document" to be interpreted according to the times we live in.

Justices Oliver Wendell Holmes (left) and Louis Brandeis (right) both fought for the rights of individuals.

Louis Brandeis

Louis Brandeis served as a justice from 1916 to 1939. He was the first Jewish person ever appointed to the Supreme Court. Brandeis had been a lawyer for nearly forty years before joining the Court. He was known as the "people's lawyer," often taking cases for free in order to help people who were poor.

Brandeis believed strongly in the fair treatment of workers. As a lawyer, he fought for shorter hours for workers, who often slaved ten or twelve hours a day. He also sought better wages for workers, and worked to protect the rights of women.

Felix Frankfurter was a Supreme Court justice for more than twenty years.

As a Court justice, Brandeis continued to uphold the rights of workers. Although some business leaders disagreed with his views, they respected him for his fair judgment and sincerity.

Felix Frankfurter

Felix Frankfurter joined the Court after being a law professor at Harvard University for twenty-five years. He was appointed by President Franklin Roosevelt in 1939 and remained on the Court until 1962.

Frankfurter gained a reputation for being very independent and fair-minded. He understood that the law was a complicated matter. If it were simple, he once said, we could do without judges. Frankfurter also felt strongly about his views. He once read a dissenting opinion with such emotion that the chief justice had to ask him to calm down.

Thurgood Marshall

In 1967, President Lyndon B. Johnson appointed Thurgood Marshall a Supreme Court justice. Marshall became the first African American to sit on the Court. Previously, he had been known as an outstanding civil rights lawyer. He won one of the Court's most famous cases—*Brown* v. *Board of Education*.

Marshall served as a lower court judge before joining the Supreme Court. On the Court, Marshall demanded that justice be upheld for all Americans. He often urged the other justices to apply their highest standards of fairness when making a decision.

Sandra Day O'Connor

When Sandra Day O'Connor joined the Supreme Court, she broke a 192-year-old male tradition. O'Connor became the first woman to serve on the Court. President Reagan appointed her in 1981.

    Before becoming a Supreme Court justice, O'Connor held many other important positions. She worked as a lawyer before becoming a senator in Arizona. She also served as a lower court judge. As a member of the Supreme Court, O'Connor quickly became known as a wise and fair individual.

Sandra Day O'Connor was the first woman to serve on the Supreme Court. Another woman, Ruth Bader Ginsburg, joined her in October 1993.

CHAPTER

5

FAMOUS RULINGS
OF THE COURT

Since its beginning, the Supreme Court has handed down thousands of decisions. All, of course, have been important. But some are better known than others because of their impact on American society.

School Integration:
Brown v. *Board of Education of Topeka*

Before the 1950s, it was legal in the United States to force non-white children to attend different schools from those of white children. In 1951, an African American named Oliver Brown sued the school board in Topeka, Kansas. He wanted his daughter Linda to attend an all-white public school near their home. He didn't want her to travel to the all-black school that was farther away.

Opposite:
Thurgood Marshall (center) leaves the Supreme Court building in May 1954, with attorneys George Hayes (left) and James Nabrit (right). The Court ruled that segregation was unconstitutional as a result of the *Brown* v. *Board of Education of Topeka* case.

This case finally reached the Supreme Court. The lawyer who represented the Browns at the hearing was Thurgood Marshall. In 1954, the Court ruled that having segregated, or separate, schools for blacks and whites was unconstitutional. By declaring this, the Court reversed a previous decision. In 1896, in a case called *Plessy* v. *Ferguson*, the Supreme Court had said there could be "separate but equal" facilities for blacks and whites. But the Court changed its mind. It said that the idea of "separate but equal" schools was unconstitutional. It went against the Fourteenth Amendment, which gives all citizens equal protection under the law.

As a result of this ruling, other civil rights changes soon followed. The Supreme Court declared that there could not be any segregated buses, hotels, restaurants, movie theaters, elevators, or other public places.

School Prayer: *Engel* v. *Vitale*

Before the 1960s, children who attended most public schools said their prayers at the start of each day. In 1962, students in New Hyde Park, New York, were ordered by their local Board of Education to say a prayer in their classroom. Some of the parents protested this act, including Stephen Engel. He decided to sue the school board, whose president was William Vitale, Jr.

After losing in a lower court, Engel appealed his case in the Supreme Court. It ruled in his favor, saying

A DOUBLE DECISION

Many Supreme Court cases deal with a single question. But occasionally a case is more involved. It requires the justices to make more than one decision. Such was the case in an important 1978 Supreme Court ruling called *Regents of the University of California* v. *Allan Bakke.*

In 1973, Allan Bakke, a white student, applied to medical school at the University of California. He was turned down. In 1974, Bakke applied again and was again rejected. Later Bakke learned that his grades and test scores were higher than those of other students who were admitted to the school. Those students had been accepted as part of a special university program to help minorities. The program was called "affirmative action."

Bakke sued the University of California. He argued that while affirmative action helped minorities, it was unfair to white males. A lower court agreed. It ordered the university to accept Bakke as a student.

The University of California appealed the case to the Supreme Court. In 1978, the Court gave an unusual two-part decision. First, it agreed that the University of California's program was illegal and ordered Bakke to be admitted to the medical school. But it also declared that schools could still consider race or ethnic background when admitting students. The strange "double ruling" caused much confusion. As a result, the question of affirmative action is still argued today in courts across the country.

that public schools cannot require students to say prayers. The Supreme Court declared this practice to be unconstitutional, because it did not keep church and state separate. The First Amendment of the Constitution says: "Congress shall make no law respecting an establishment of religion."

A Suspect's Rights: *Miranda v. Arizona*

In 1963, Ernesto Miranda was arrested in Arizona. He was suspected of several serious crimes. The police questioned him for two hours. But they did not tell him he had the right to remain silent or to see a lawyer. Later, Miranda signed a written confession.

Ernesto Miranda's case resulted in new guidelines for arrest procedures of suspected criminals.

At his trial, Miranda took back his confession, but the jury still found him guilty. In 1966, the Supreme Court reviewed his case. It reversed the earlier decision. In a later trial, Miranda was again found guilty, but this verdict was based on other evidence, not on his confession.

Today, people who are arrested must always be read their rights before they are questioned. Otherwise, statements made by the suspects cannot be used as evidence in court.

Book Banning: *Board of Education* v. *Pico*

In 1975, a school board in Long Island, New York, ordered nine books removed from its schools' library shelves. It said the books were "anti-American, anti-Christian, anti-Semitic, and just plain filthy." Students at the schools, including one named Steven Pico, sued. They claimed that their First Amendment rights were being denied.

A lower court first ruled in favor of the school board. Then, a higher court ruled in favor of the students. The case was then appealed for the second time. Finally, in 1982, the Supreme Court upheld the higher court's ruling. It said that a school board could not remove a library's books simply because it didn't like the ideas presented in them.

Flag Burning: *Texas* v. *Johnson*

In 1984, during a Republican party convention in Dallas, Texas, Gregory Lee Johnson burned the American flag as a protest. He was convicted of violating a state law against destroying a symbolic object and sentenced to prison. After a higher court reversed the ruling, the case went to the Supreme Court.

In 1989, the Supreme Court declared that the First Amendment protects a person's right to burn the American flag. It also said the government cannot stop someone from expressing a personal or political view just because other people find that view offensive.

Gregory Johnson, arrested for flag burning in 1989, holds a U.S. flag. The Supreme Court ruled that flag burning is protected by the First Amendment of the Constitution.

Other Supreme Court Rulings

In years past, there have been thousands of other important Supreme Court rulings. They relate to many difficult questions, such as:

- What is a newspaper or magazine allowed to publish?
- For what reasons may a company fire someone?
- Can a religious symbol be displayed in public?
- Can immigrants be kept from entering the United States?
- What cannot be said on radio or shown on TV?
- Should minorities be given preference in job hiring?
- Can a student's locker be searched without permission?

It is important for you to know about Supreme Court decisions because many of them may have a direct impact on you in some way. Some of them may affect you while in school, and others when you take a job. Supreme Court decisions are ones that all Americans must obey. They are also decisions that you have the power to try to change through amendments to the Constitution.

For more than two centuries, the Supreme Court of the United States has helped to shape America through its rulings. It has sought to guarantee that our nation's laws remain fair, according to the ideas in the Constitution. Today, the Supreme Court continues to uphold the rights and freedoms of all American citizens.

Chronology

1787	American leaders create the U.S. Constitution.
1790	The Supreme Court meets for the first time.
1793	The Supreme Court hands down its first major ruling.
1801	The Supreme Court moves from Philadelphia to Washington, D.C.
1803	In *Marbury* v. *Madison*, John Marshall declares the Supreme Court can overrule a law of Congress.
1857	In the Dred Scott case, the Supreme Court rules that slaves are considered property and that African Americans, slaves or free, can never be U.S. citizens. The ruling helps lead to the Civil War.
1898	In *Plessy* v. *Ferguson*, the Court says that blacks and whites may have "separate but equal" facilities.
1920	The Nineteenth Amendment is ratified, giving women the right to vote.
1935	The Supreme Court building is established.
1952	The Supreme Court rules that an order made by President Harry S. Truman is unconstitutional.
1954	In *Brown* v. *Board of Education of Topeka*, the Court reverses its previous decision. It now says "separate but equal" schools cannot exist.
1962	In *Engel* v. *Vitale*, the Court says that public schools cannot require students to say prayers.
1967	Thurgood Marshall becomes the first African American to join the Court.
1971	The Twenty-sixth Amendment secures the vote for all citizens over 18.
1981	Sandra Day O'Connor is the first woman to join the Court.
1982	In *Board of Education* v. *Pico*, the Court rules that a school board cannot ban books from a school library.
1989	In *Texas* v. *Johnson*, the Supreme Court rules that the First Amendment protects a person's right to burn the American flag.

For Further Reading

Coy, Harold. *The Supreme Court.* New York: Franklin Watts, 1981.

Gherman, Beverly. *Sandra Day O'Connor.* New York: Viking, 1991.

Greene, Carol. *The Supreme Court.* Chicago: Childrens Press, 1985.

Jenkins, George. *Constitution.* Vero Beach, Florida: Rourke Publishing, 1990.

Lawson, Don. *Landmark Supreme Court Cases.* Hillside, New Jersey: Enslow Publishers, 1987.

Stein, R. Conrad. *The Story of the Powers of the Supreme Court.* Chicago: Childrens Press, 1989.

Weiss, Ann E. *The Supreme Court.* Hillside, New Jersey: Enslow Publishers, 1987.

Index

Adams, John, 16

Blackmun, Harry S., 21, 32
Board of Education v. *Pico*, 43
Bork, Robert, 32
Brandeis, Louis, 24, 35–36
Brown v. *Board of Education*, 36, 39–40
Brown, Oliver, 39

Chase, Salmon, 22
Civil War, 19, 20
Constitution, 4, 5, 8, 9, 16, 18, 24, 26, 33, 35
    amendments to, 12–13, 16, 20, 40, 41, 43
    Article III of, 7, 16

Dartmouth College Case, The, 19
Dred Scott v. *Sandford*, 19–20

Engel, Stephen, 40
Engel v. *Vitale*, 40–41
"Equal Justice Under Law," 7, 29

Frankfurter, Felix, 36

Gibbons v. *Ogden*, 19
Ginsburg, Ruth Bader, 21, 37
Government, branches of, 12

Hayes, George, 39
Holmes, Oliver Wendell, 10, 35
House of Representatives, 12, 33

Jay, John, 33–34
Jefferson, Thomas, 17
Johnson, Gregory Lee, 43, 44
Johnson, Lyndon B., 36

Kennedy, Anthony M., 21, 32

Madison, James, 17
Marbury v. *Madison,* 16–18, 19
Marbury, William, 16–18
Marshall, John, 14, 16, 17–18, 34
Marshall, Thurgood, 36, 38, 40
Miranda v. *Arizona*, 42
Miranda, Ernesto, 42

Nabrit, James, 39
Nixon, Richard, 11, 32

O'Connor, Sandra Day, 21, 37

Pico, Steven, 43
Plessy v. *Ferguson*, 40

Reagan, Ronald, 37
Regents of California v. *Allan Bakke*, 41
Rehnquist, William, 21
Roosevelt, Franklin, 21, 36
Royal Exchange Building, 20

Scalia, Antonin, 21
Scott, Dred, 19, 20
Senate, 5, 12, 31, 32, 33
Souter, David H., 21
Stevens, John Paul, 21
Suffragettes, 13
Supreme Court
    calendar of, 28–29
    cases before, 24
    decisions of, 11, 24–25, 39–45
    job of, 8
    judicial review of, 18
    justices, 21, 30
    requirements to, 31, 32
    start of, 15–16
Supreme Court building, 6, 29
    history of, 20
    interior chamber of, 5, 28

Taney, Roger B., 19
Texas v. *Johnson*, 43
Thomas, Clarence, 21
Truman, Harry S., 11

U.S. Court of Appeals, 11, 26
United State Reports, 25

Vitale, William, Jr., 40

Warren, Earl, 34
Washington, George, 15, 33

48

BENNETT-HEMENWAY
SCHOOL LIBRARY
NATICK, MA

347.9
G

Goldish, Meish

Our Supreme Court

MAY 2 3 2009	DATE DUE		
MAY 0 6 2009			

BENNETT-HEMENWAY
SCHOOL LIBRARY
NATICK, MA